A Collection of Poems

by

Louise Archer

Published by New Generation Publishing in 2020

Copyright © Louise Archer 2020

First Edition

The author asserts the moral right under the Copyright, Designs and Patents Act 1988 to be identified as the author of this work.

All Rights reserved. No part of this publication may be reproduced, stored in a retrieval system or transmitted, in any form or by any means without the prior consent of the author, nor be otherwise circulated in any form of binding or cover other than that which it is published and without a similar condition being imposed on the subsequent purchaser.

ISBN
        Paperback   978-1-80031-694-2
        Hardback   978-1-80031-693-5

www.newgeneration-publishing.com

This book is a love song to my family and friends and an expression in part of the joy of nature.

People

Journey

For Stuart

We travel alone most days

Searching for the flicker of recognition

To ease our pain and keep us sane;

We are helpless and love in desperate measure,

to build against the cold tide of age.

Sometimes our beauty is lost,

our hope destroyed, but we go on

probing the depths of our soul for

new light on the harsh reality of life.

To each new day we add our colour

and see ourselves fade

in the mists of time.

This race we cannot win,

but we must try

to burn our love upon this space and

leave a glow of inspiration for

those who follow on.

Wedding Poem

For Stuart and Pauline

My love for you
is in the everyday
and the spectacular.
In a quiet smile
or sudden gesture.
I am content to
know you are beside me,
that your happiness
and sorrow can guide me.
In shared sunsets
and laughter
bright days
or disaster.
In caution or impulse
Unchanging and constant,
in inspiration or anger.

My love for you
wraps moments of joy
like jewels in the sea.
Our ebb and our flow
is what matters to me.
To hold you through the tests of time
and know that I am better
for your love
and you for mine.

Father

I touch the hearth
The hearth you sat beside so long
while my life moved on.
In my mind I could always
see you there.
An anchor for wherever
I was.
I look back and imagine your
arms as a frame around
the fields of daises where
me and my sisters had lain.
Keeping us safe with
your care and love
watching out for all of us.
I miss your knowledge,
the sound advice.
The quiet way you
helped me in my life.
You are present still
in my heart,
but how I wish you were
still sat beside the hearth.

Eva

I see you kneeling on the lawn

it is a wonder to us all,

this small plot of paradise

created by your loving hands.

And where you're gone

I feel I know, you'll find

a way to make thing grow.

May you find peace in your garden above.

Good memories will comfort us.

and in our hearts

the lasting love

for all you gave.

Nicole

Beloved sister don't you know

just how much I love you so

like the blossom on the trees

we fade with time

but you will be

blooming in my heart

for all eternity.

Matthew

You taught us grace
and every time your mother spoke
a smile lit up your face,
wide as the ocean.

We could not know
your thoughts or dreams
but it seemed
you were content.

Surrounded by love
and happy days
you did not complain
in any way.

We were blessed
to have you in our lives
And in our hearts,
you'll always be alive.

For Joshua (written in Le Hocq)

The storm raged for hours,

flashes of lightening

like someone taking a

photograph repeatedly.

Tonight we should see

the meteor shower

but I can only hear

the leaves rustling

in the trees

and distant thunder.

I wait to see you home.

My soulful child,

my son.

James

Shining star,

hope of mine.

Reason for living,

you make it alright.

How can I say,

what I want you to know.

The words they just seem

to come out wrong.

I give you my heart.

You're so

Not what I planned
or expected
Not romantic
or tactile
sometimes anxious
and facile.

Not cheery and fun
introverted and wan
quiet and distant
Not noisy and instant.

Yet here we are
over twenty years on
we found a way
and time has gone.

We share a love
of creativity
You obsess about music
more explicitly.

We both like art
and comedy,
though our knowledge
is quite limited.

You're not what I planned
or expected
I've said it before,
it's not new.
So here we are, me being me
and you being you.

For Janet and Paul

Your eyes light up when you see me,

with love and hope.

A small smile moves across my lips.

Your kindness disarmed me

You seemed to understand

my darker moments, could

hold them in your hand.

Simple pleasures abound and

you have learned not to frown

too much at my untidiness.

We must bless the days,

rich with warmth and laughter.

Gather precious memories

for ever after.

CJ

There's a girl with fire in her eyes,
golden blonde with a wicked smile.
Watch her making the world turn around,
there's always laughter to be found.

There's a girl with passion her heart,
who never gives in when times are hard.
She's wiser now than she was before
but that just makes you love her more.

For Max

My autumn friend,

strong as a tree

restless as the wind.

Drink with me

to life and happiness.

Hold this moment

in your memory.

And as we wind our way

through life's complexities

remember we can shape

our own destiny.

And write in colours

bold and clear

our history.

Dear Mr Hockney

We came to see your work

and watched you on the culture show.

I wanted you to know

you inspired me to write this verse.

The paintings of the countryside

opened wide my memories

of being young,

of endless fields in the sun,

running round, having fun.

It is a wonderful legacy

that you will leave

capturing the changing seasons

and the trees

that still us all when we reflect,

 the joys of nature

are the best.

Auden

Had I never seen
the deep etched lines
of your lived in face
I may have never been sustained.

You have been there as solace
In the dark and brightest days
to temper my ambition
and sit with contrition
on the brow of my pauses.

My only regret, no chance
to meet and find you forgettable.
Although it goes without saying,
the likelihood is very small
that I could ever forget you at all.

Your words on my lips
like greasy chips that
I wipe away but still taste.
I touch your books for comfort
And think of times you brought
a spark to the dry tinder of my heart.

The Ballad of Laura Loosely

She wore black on a Sunday
to mourn her father's death.
He died at the great hall table
laughing with his last breath.

All through the week
she quietly sat
looking down at the river
on Friday she donned her blue party dress
and danced alone like a lover.

Her name was Laura Loosley
She wore a bridal gown
On occasional Saturday evenings
when she wandered into town.

She stood beneath the clocktower
and silently she cried
Why of why did he have to die
she often said out loud.

To the idle passer by
it seemed her father's loss
Was the reason she cried out in pain
but a few knew it was not.

For Laura Loosley was to wed
a gentleman form the south.
She sent him love tokens every day
once kissed him on the mouth.

In September '43 she waited at the church
Her hair bright with golden roses
that captured the morning light.
No man came to stand beside her,
her father took her arm.
She did not weep or speak a word
as he led her back to the car.

The war had taken her love,
like the leaves that blew away
covering the ground in the churchyard
on that fateful day.

Seasons

The day seems suspended

The air is still

The light of early evening

shades the day.

This is the edge of summer

A promise of warm days.

I lift my eyes to the sky

And raise my head hopeful

about what is left of the year.

The light draws me in.

The last energy of spring is making

my heart light with

the possibility of things to come.

The trees heavy with blossom

sing of summer coming

Blue skies and sun.

The bees have begun

to search for pollen.

Honey to be made.

Sweet nights and days.

The hedgerows weighed with their gifts

The air scented and still.

Green lanes winding

through the countryside.

Boats on the canal

A distant church bell

echoing across the morning

I am reminded of childhood walks,

the joy of discovery

of nature.

No sense of hurry,

time to wander

enjoy the wonder.

March 2013

It's snowing, small flakes
in the cold wind.
Winter seems not to be ending.
People going by bend in against
the bad weather.
Others looking out wonder
when it will get better.
On the news they say
the coldest March since 1962.
What can we do
but wait for spring?
The daffodils are out
a bright splash against the day.
We have to be grateful for
it's warm indoors and
with a steaming mug of tea
we can refresh ourselves and
plan for warmer days.
All things pass, the snow will
not last forever.

Rain

Rain, rain

heavy rain

streaming down the window panes

drowning out other sounds.

Like millions of tears all around.

Christmas Day 2010

We are strong and
we are blessed
When everything is
stripped away
what we have left
is love.
We are strong and
we are blessed.

NYE 2008

On New Year's Eve,

in my bunny ears

the love and the fireworks

bring me to tears.

Places

Commuting

On the morning shuttle
it's delight upon the eye
to see the swans at Eastleigh
as we go hurtling by.
England's green and pleasant land
hurries by at who's command.
As we near Southampton water
the sea calls out to those before her
urging all to leave and see
the wonders of the world, be free.
Ships and trains and planes go by
but I am pleased to stay awhile.
Reflecting on the rolling views,
untouched by ever changing news.
Fold away the world today,
start seeing in a different way.

Wedmore

Swallows at the end of summer

swoosh across the sky.

Horses blink their soulful eyes.

The ginger cat follows us

down the lane.

Clouds roll in with gentle rain.

The weather vane is still

as we look towards the hills.

Not far away the sea,

promises possibilities.

Some cities

I remembered the greyness of them

not a cold grey, solid grey, safe grey,

I wanted to reach out and touch.

Mingling with the mist of morning

Coughing into life in sprawling silence.

Unseen life hurrying between

the dark and light.

Moved by the dawn, edged with the night.

Such desolation, dressed in hope.

Grabbing the sun from its cloud stricken blight.

Dust framed window-blinking eye like

upon the same picture, unchanging

yet changed so subtly we cannot tell.

Bright steeped autumn splendour.

Evolved in time but frozen

In my mind eye forever burning.

Syria-(Peace Plan 12.04.2012)

No-one died today,
running in the streets
holding their beliefs
like armour.
This peace is fragile
and while the world watches
plans will be made.
The protests won't fade.
The air is fraught with grief.
Tears fall on the dusty ground
for all those lost in search of freedom.
Fleeing the destruction
some cross the border
leaving behind once
ordinary lives and order.
And we in the west
who may think we know best
may not understand
the complexities of this land.
We have our rights and
at least can understand
the fight to stop oppression.
To live without fear
with all we hold dear beside us.

Love and relationships

Transit of Venus-06.06.2012

Love has gone by

Across the sky

We won't see this again

in our lifetime.

If love is past

what do we have that lasts?

Maybe our search

Must go beyond the earth.

Can we wait for love to come back?

Or create something

in it's track.

Love has gone by.

Across the sky.

We must not wonder why

at this wonder in the sky.

We must hold it's sight

and make new light.

Softly enclosing

your arms like a harbour

safe from the storm

I lay beside you

in shelter and warmth.

While the night rages

the torment of ages

casts for my attention

in dreams more relentless.

You stop and capture

held close in rapture

beside smiles and laughter

release form the day.

Melt away pain

float gently together

like tides overlapping

mixed into each other

one rhythm forever

on the crest of the twilight

as blue becomes midnight

and hush whispers over the spirits of light.

And when I dreamed
your bronzed arm reached me
pulled me back
across the fear of distance
your hot breath on my body
between the summer sheets of blue
we made our promises
now winter's ice has forgotten
the bleak stained window
holds no reminder of spent passion
and I alone recall the fire that
burned within our room
delirious with love.

Love comes slowly sometimes

and leaves suddenly.

Taking us by surprise,

like a change in the colour of the skies.

We may wonder why

it took so long to realise

or how it went

like an impatient traveller

who leaves at night

never to return.

All I cannot know

I saw you in a dream last night
when I was raging with pain.
I haven't come to terms yet
with not seeing you again.
I caught your laughter in a moment
off guard I can't forget,
trying to put the sadness
into some perspective.
As I run along,
to escape the hurt
I know I'll have to backtrack
to deal with it some more.
Each day I'll be stronger
as time moves on.
Asking can we really choose
when we have so much to lose.
Are we alone, do we belong
only when we choose to go beyond
the raw emotion.
Do you understand now
all the things I cannot know.
Will these wounds heal and
your love let me go.

Love to love

Love bites back
It has that knack.
You try to squash it
into hate.
It just smiles
like the hand of fate
on your shoulder.
Love is bolder
won't let you go,
Seems to know
you need it
Don't want it.
It's not going to stop.
Don't stand a chance
when love wants to dance.
Find yourself moving
when love comes grooving.
It keeps coming back
and has the last laugh.

Life

Life is a sweater unravelling,

I am wool

you are string

you tie me up

and wait for me

to bring

Love unconditional.

Lightning Source UK Ltd.
Milton Keynes UK
UKHW010258090223
416650UK00003B/871